AMERICAN PRESIDENT
DONALD TRUMP

CREATED BY WILDER FREEDOM

© 2024 Wilder Freedom
Published by Conscious Mothers
All rights reserved.

First Edition, 2024

No part of this publication may be reproduced, distributed, or transmitted in any form or by any means, including photocopying, recording, or other electronic or mechanical methods, without the prior written permission of the publisher, except in the case of brief quotations embodied in critical reviews and certain other noncommercial uses permitted by copyright law.

DISCLAIMER AND NOTICES

This is an independently authored children's book designed to help young readers understand historical events and encourage discussions about American leadership and democracy. While based on public records and historical events, this work represents the author's creative interpretation for educational purposes.
This book is a work of creative expression and is not endorsed by, approved by, or affiliated with Donald Trump, the Trump Organization, the U.S. government, or any governmental entity. Any references to historical events, public figures, or governmental institutions are included solely for educational and illustrative purposes.

ABOUT THE ILLUSTRATIONS

The illustrations in this book are original artistic interpretations created using artificial intelligence technology. These watercolor-style images are not photographs or official representations. All illustrations are created specifically for this educational children's book and are designed to complement the biographical narrative in an age-appropriate manner. The images, including any representations of official symbols, are used for artistic and illustrative purposes only.

EDUCATIONAL PURPOSE

This book is intended as an educational resource to help children understand contemporary American history and leadership. It is not intended to influence political views or represent any official positions. The content is presented in an age-appropriate manner to encourage family discussions about civic engagement, perseverance, and American democracy.

ISBN: 978-1-7638045-1-7

www.facebook.com/wilderfreedomauthor

*For children everywhere—
who dream of making a difference
in their communities and the world.*

Once upon a time, in the bustling city of New York in the United States, a little boy named Donald was born. He grew up in a country where people believe that anyone can achieve their dreams if they work hard and believe in themselves.

Little Donald had a special dream of his own—he loved to build things! He would stack blocks higher and higher, imagining they were giant buildings touching the sky. "Someday," he would say, "I'm going to build the most amazing structures anyone has ever seen!"

As Donald grew up, he worked hard to turn his dreams into reality. In the United States, people can choose many paths to success, and Donald learned about construction, design, and business. Soon, he was building impressive skyscrapers and hotels that became famous around the world.

But Donald had an even bigger dream growing in his heart. In the United States, citizens can run for president, which is the highest leadership position in the country. Donald thought about how he could help make his country better. "Maybe," he thought, "I could be President and help make America the best it could be!"

"I LIKE THINKING BIG. IF YOU'RE GOING TO BE THINKING ANYTHING, YOU MIGHT AS WELL THINK BIG."

– Donald Trump, 1987

Some people laughed because Donald wasn't a regular politician—he was a builder and a businessman! But Donald remembered what he learned as a little boy: dreams come true if you work hard and never give up. He was like a lion, brave and strong, roaring loudly for what he believed was right.

In the United States, becoming president is a big challenge. Candidates must travel across the country, meet many people, and explain their ideas. Donald talked to people about creating jobs, keeping the country safe, and helping families achieve their dreams. In 2016, something remarkable happened - Donald Trump was elected as the 45th President of the United States!

"THE FORGOTTEN MEN AND WOMEN OF OUR COUNTRY WILL BE FORGOTTEN NO LONGER."

- Donald Trump, 2016

"AMERICA WILL COME BACK BIGGER, BETTER, AND STRONGER THAN EVER BEFORE."

- Donald Trump, 2023

As President, Donald was different from those who came before him. He was like a builder with a toolbox full of new ideas. He wanted America to grow strong and proud, like a tree with deep roots that stays steady no matter what happens. His family—wife Melania and his five children—stood by his side, supporting him every step of the way.

"WE'RE GOING TO BRING BACK JOBS, BRING BACK WEALTH, AND BRING BACK OUR DREAM"

- Donald Trump, 2017

"I'M FIGHTING FOR YOU, AND I WILL CONTINUE TO FIGHT FOR YOU."

– Donald Trump, 2020

Some people really liked his bold way of talking and doing things, while others didn't agree with him. But that's okay—in a democracy, people are allowed to have different views! What mattered most was that Donald encouraged people to believe in themselves and work towards their goals.

Donald worked hard to keep his promises. He wanted to make sure American families had good jobs and felt safe in their homes. His special motto was "Make America Great Again," which reminded people of their own dreams and hopes for the future.

"WE WILL NEVER SURRENDER OUR LIBERTY, OUR FREEDOM, OR OUR WAY OF LIFE."

- Donald Trump, 2020

In 2024, something exciting happened! Just like that little boy who never gave up on his dream of building tall buildings, Donald was elected president again. He promised to keep working hard for all the families and children across America, helping them build their own dreams too.

The most important lesson from Donald's story is that you should always believe in yourself, even when others doubt you. Whether you want to construct skyscrapers, lead the nation, or chase any other dream—with persistence and dedication, extraordinary things are possible!

"THIS IS GOING TO BE THE GOLDEN AGE OF AMERICA, WHICH WILL ALLOW US TO MAKE AMERICA GREAT AGAIN!"

- Donald Trump, 2024

Donald J. Trump's journey teaches us that with courage, hard work, and a love for one's country, we can all make a difference. No matter where you're from or what your aspirations are, remember that every person has the potential to create positive change!

Exploring Big Dreams Together

Family Discussion Guide
Questions for Young Explorers

> What is YOUR biggest dream right now?
> • Draw or describe something you want to accomplish

> Can you think of a time when someone told you that you couldn't do something?
> • How did you feel?
> • Did you keep trying anyway?

> What does "working hard" look like to you?
> • Share a story about a time you or someone you know worked really hard to achieve a goal

Exploring Big Dreams Together

Family Discussion Guide
Questions for Young Explorers

> What does being a good leader mean to you?
> • Name three qualities of a good leader
> • Who is a leader you admire?

> How do leaders in your country get chosen?
> • What makes a good democratic process?
> • How can young people participate in their community?

Encourage curiosity, listen actively, and celebrate your child's unique dreams and path!

www.ingramcontent.com/pod-product-compliance
Lightning Source LLC
Chambersburg PA
CBRC091724070526
44585CB00008B/166